Thirty Year Blend ℂ
Rick

All rights reserved.

No part of this publication may be reproduced, stored in a retrieval system, or transmitted, in any form or by any means, electronic, mechanical, photocopying, recording or otherwise, without the prior written permission of the presenters.

B. Kamilah Ricketts asserts the moral right to be identified as author of this work.

Presentation by *BookLeaf Publishing*

Web: www.bookleafpub.com

E-mail: info@bookleafpub.com

ISBN: 9789357612944

First edition 2022

Thirty Year Blend

B. Kamilah Ricketts

to young Breezzy & Rez Lamar

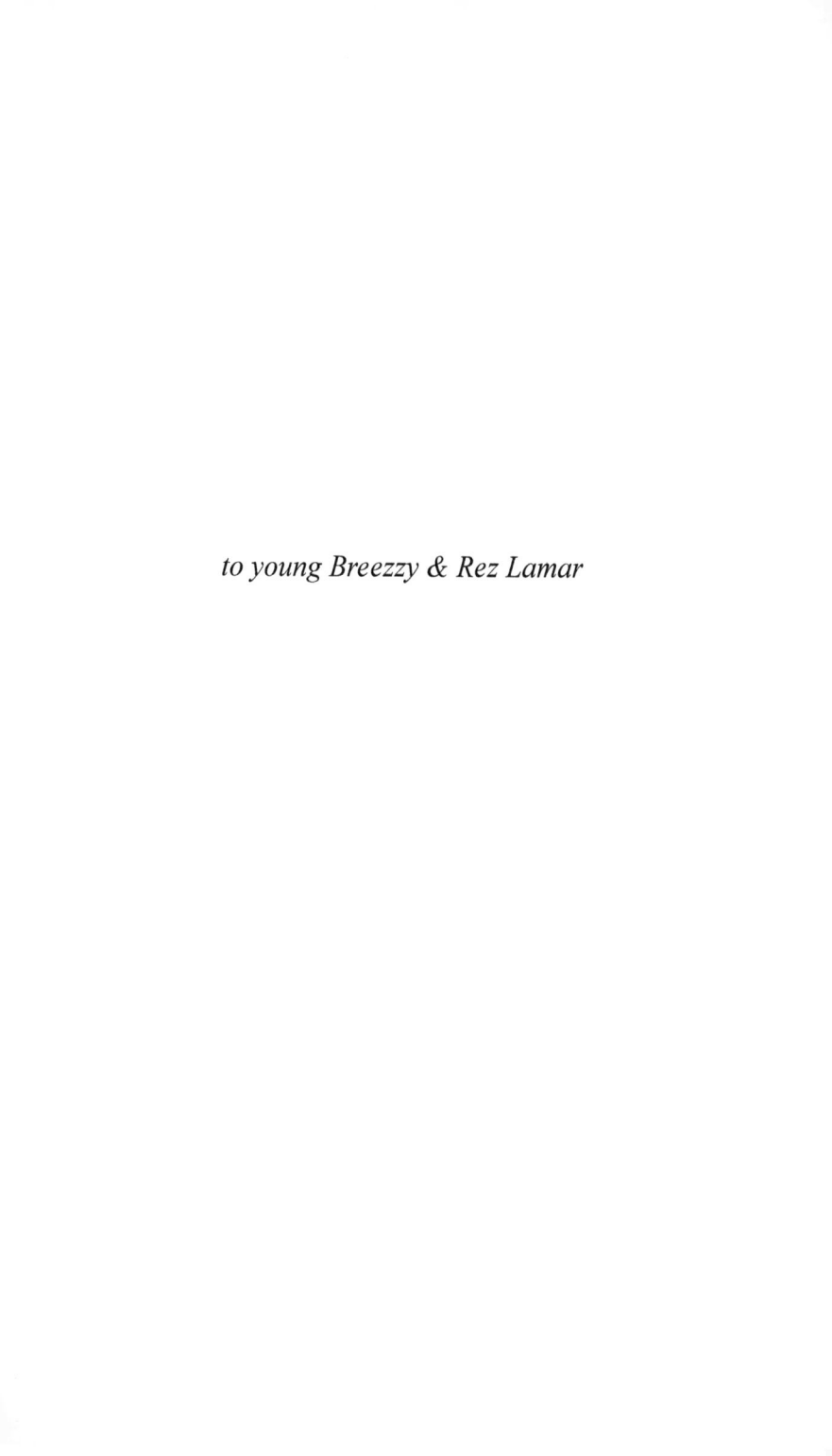

ACKNOWLEDGEMENT

I would first like to acknowledge my family who saw my gift for writing and bought me countless notebooks and encouraged me to continue.

Secondly, I would like to acknowledge Professor Erica Hunt who consistently bought cake or dinner when I had a class on my birthday during grad school and couldn't celebrate otherwise.

I would also like to acknowledge Hanibel who has read every single story I've put into the world since undergrad.

Camry and Tara for noticing and admonishing me when I stopped writing.

My fiance, Odell, who nudges me to write and publish.

The LIU writing community who write every Sunday.

Lastly, every single person who has interacted, read, and supported @brickpages. You are greatly appreciated.

Bitter Grinds

I have spent years believing I was fine because
I have dug a hold in my chest that got deeper
every year
I have buried the parts I didn't like
So I can't hear me crying

And I spoke loud and laughed louder
And used my voice to advocate for the children
Because my work was more urgent & important
And I trudged through Brownsville, Brooklyn
believing I was fine.

Trying to forget about the shallow grave I dug
Waiting for the wounds to dry up or fester like
a sore or crust and sugar over
Like waiting for Godot
carrying them,
I'm a bag lady- but at least they're designer

And I would have gone on that way until I met
you
And now

I admit, they come when I least expect it
When I'm doing my hair- when I'm chilling
when I'm just loving you

When I feel the walls finally crumbling
Then it comes with its pointer finger
Knowing exactly where- boom!
There's the trigger

There are times I feel the vibes of what it must be like to be you
Getting the brunt of things
that you and I know you didn't do
And if I could control it -I wouldn't linger
I hate seeing you upset over my trigger

I think I was never taught how to let go forever
I have to remember just in case
In case it happens to me again
My body protecting me from things I can't face
I'm praying that I could be a person God will consider
when He is handing out healing for triggers

It's hard to feel like I deserve this love
with all the consistent reminders of abuse and pain
You don't deserve these random surges
I'm trying to determine if this will remain.
I know I'm strong- probably as strong as you figure
But it doesn't mean that I can handle all of these triggers.

12 Ounce Drip with Oat

Support is
remembering to deny me
when I ask for something
that will bring pain in the end

Support is
pushing me until
I feel like
I might
break
to make me feel better

Support is
carrying burdens
I got so used to carrying they
felt like
they were a part of me

Gingerbread Bread Latte

Hold on to you
because if you don't
life becomes private school lines
of plaid skirts and silent lunches

Hold on to you
if you let go
you become a lump of clay
in the hands of the masses

Love you because if you don't
pain will be the
only feeling
you'll really know

Venti White Chocolate Mocha with Almond Milk

I am mega churches
and reggae lounges
I am living in
service of others and a
selfish babe
I am a procrastinator and a
planner
I look for a seat at the table
while building my own

I am private school and public
8 am and 3 am bedtimes
An adult and a child
My trauma and my healing
I am me

Black Coffee

we wake up in the morning we
wish we could go back to bed and wear
pajamas all day. But we put on the
makeup, we put on the coffee to mask
the tiredness we feel. we cry that
we live in such a capitalist world & create grins
that a depressive episode and an
anxiety attack can't setal (we say) -its all lies

High functioning is what they call it
High key high all the time the smoke hides
the strenuousness of our
lives and we wonder: is this how it should be?
tear-stained cheeks?

And we mosey on to work and
say our affirmations & send prayers in shades
of pain asking God to change our
reality
Maybe He can adjust our eyes
to see joy
in all of this.

Double Espresso Shot

Falling in love
and getting married
is like a surreal party
they're playing your favorite artist
and you dance with one person
the whole night
with all the eye contact
and flirtatious words
then

all the rest of the party
wants to be involved and you
have to divert your eyes to
accommodate all the
feelings and voices and

you're worried you won't or
can't
get back to who you were
with your all-night dance partner-
you're real self.

"Blue Mountain Cafecito" From "The Negro Speaks of Rives" by Langston Hughes

I wonder about the things I've
seen. The people I have known
the oceans, the gullys, and rivers
I've swum in the bodies of my ancient
family members, my ancestors sitting under dusky
skies, in the Caribbean breeze watching drives
thinking about me? Wondering what my
life would be like, petitioning goddesses for my soul?

I grew older than people my age, my body has
a the same age but my soul is grown
and maybe my thoughts get too deep
trying to be like & think like
everyone my age makes my brain, the
frontal cortex cringe. I'd
rather feel deep like the Caribbean rivers.

Macchiato

Its like what kind of dumb
girl stays in a situation
where someone is purposefully hurting her
like do you love your...

> I reach out
> to feel the
> lavender in
> front of me. I
> turn around and
> I see lavender
> everywhere.
> I feel my feet
> pick up underneath
> through the fields
> feeling
> my white cotton
> dress billowing

Did you hear me?
Yeah
Oh. Okay. You were like gone for a second.

Dirty Chai

I used to hate dirt
Dirt would get on my clothes
after racing down the block
with my childhood neighbors
Dirt
would get into my cuts and scrapes
and my dad would throw peroxide
on my knees and elbows
to get it out
I would squirm and squeeze
my eyes shut
and one day when I opened them
it was still dark

the darkness followed me
for a while
and I cried and screamed until
I realized I was there to grow

I felt myself sprouting
roots and I
pushed and prodded until I found
myself facing the sun

and then I was thankful for the dirt
it helped me grow

Mocha

Only you can love me
Deeply enough to reach me
Even when I feel
Lower than the Earth
Love that reaches the end of this world

Affogato

The day of my birth
28 years ago that time
there was the ticking of
the clock growing louder as
2 former boys I used to know called
to wish me a happy trip around the sun
triggered me to cry tears as large as grapes
realizing how dry of a situation
I was in and my goal of 25 and married
was a distant memory
I cried because their efforts were meager
and my standards had dropped to
my wooden floors

that day I cried and
I wailed with the sky
but it was a cleansing cry because with it
I picked up my pride
I picked up my elegance
I picked up my Queendom

Pumkin Spice Latte

Happy Birthday wherever you
are I hope you're happy too.
when we were younger
and life was simpler
being friends was just easier
shit got too complicated
and I'm sad we didn't make it
I'm getting married in 38 days
I wish you could be there in some way
But on your birthday I hope

I hope the sadness that would
take over your body be no more
And that after 30 years your
karma finally comes through for you
I hope you got your vegan pumpkin cheesecake
that you made some friends you trust
and that you're experiencing real love

Sorrel & Turkey

When I think of you
I'll remember a peacemaker
The epitome of
can we all just get along
I think of 48-hour soaks
for hibiscus leaves
for the last Thursday in November

I'll remember
big laughs and weight checks
Your melodic way of
talking & always feeling a
little better when I would
leave your house on the corner
in Baisley park

I'll remember thinking your name
Joy
was always so fitting
Because you were Joy even when the family
felt like enemies
You were Joy even when things felt odd
around the holiday table

Joy that will never be hidden under a bushel.
Joy that we'll never forget.

Latte Macchiato

I never was afraid of ghosts.
I believed in life after the grave
I believed in angels and demons that take
different hosts
But ghosts- they've never put fear in my heart

Until you.

You walked out in the middle of our duet
Left me singing solo, and I
Kept singing
waiting, hoping one day you'd join me again

After one year I realized you weren't coming
back
I had to end the song on my own.
And so along with visible demons and angels,
Ghosts quickly became the thing I fear the most.

CAPiccino

I'm a movement by myself
But I'm a force when we're together
Mami, I'm good all by myself
you, you make me better

I'm a force when we're together
I did not ask for this
you, you make me better
Even if you can't see who you're with

I did not ask for this
You and your commitment and all this pressure
Even if you can't see who you're with
I know that I do things for my pleasure

You and your commitment and all this pressure
"for me to be better" you keep crying and
I know I do things for my pleasure
I'm not ready. I'm not trying.

"for me to be better" you keep crying and
Baby, I know what we could be - but
I know I do things for my pleasure
I don't want to hurt you so I'm keeping it a buck

Baby, I know what we could be - but

I'm a movement by myself
I don't want to hurt you, so I'm keeping it a buck
Mami, I'm good all by myself

Dalgona Coffee

Take it slow-
slow-
slow-
you're an alto sax and
I'm an electric guitar
Me in an open field in Prospect park
and dark intimate jazz club for you.
And sometimes the sounds we make together
Cause my chest to tighten and my legs to quake
Because you- and I-
we walk to different beats
and maybe we can make each other better
if we learn each other and take it slow
slow-
slow- it's time we take it slow.

Ristretto

I am Breana
I am Strong.
Not in the way you planned.
I carry the weight of sins against me
Cha-em-wese.
it has molded me to be strong-willed
created someone Strong Minded
Someone who does not Need anyone else
but craves love unconditional.
Brick Walls protecting Wine Glasses
Teflon Feathers
i am strong.

Lungo

Its October 27th
I decided to spend this weekend at a friend's house
We promised to spend every weekend together
I didn't want to be alone
you wanted to go out with friends
so I went out with mine
Hurricane Sandy is coming
All I wonder is when will I see you again?

It's October 28th
I'm looking on my smartphone
The storm is underway
My New York is drowning
Sharks are swimming around the Jersey shore
You're only a tunnel and a few highways away
But it feels like you're worlds away
Now I'm wondering, will I see you again?

Its October 30th
We've been arguing every day
You never call
I always call
Empty apologies
Empty I love yous
I'm in my warm and cozy room

Feeling cold and empty inside
Do I even want to see you again?

When Sandy came she didn't just breeze through
She took our warmth
She took our light
She rampaged through my life
Sandy ruined our plans
And now I'm wondering if you ever want to see me again.

Caramel Ribbon Crunch Frapuccino

"Write about us"

Write about us, you say, as if it is that simple. We are not simple. We are complex and beautiful and easy, but how do I put us on paper?

I feel my cellular data changing, my real self fighting to come to the surface. The nine-year-old who was unafraid, soft, and bubbly.

All of a sudden- I'm not too nice, I'm not too American, I'm not too Jamaican, I'm not too dark to be Cuban, I am not too proper, I'm not too weird, I'm not too smart. I'm not too Christian. My laugh isn't too loud. My arms aren't too fat. I am not too much. I can just be?

What the fuck am I supposed to do with that?

Somehow I'm more than enough and never too much. Doing what comes naturally to me isn't overkill. I'm not "doing too much for someone who doesn't deserve it" … because you do?

I was dropped in the Garden of Eden and let free. But I'm scared to walk in. Hanging out by the entrance. Surrounded by Monarchs, Peonies, Cardinals, and Prunus trees but I'm trying to peek around the bend, trying to see how it ends. I've never been here before. What the fuck do I do here?

I hear you pleading "Let me love you!" questioning "Are you going to let me love you?"

I'm over here trying to figure out how. How do I reprogram myself to let you love me? What happens if I let myself get vulnerable? Truly vulnerable? Like behind the wall I built when I was 10? Who is that person? Would I still be loved?

You mean, I don't have to protect my heart because you'll actually be careful with it for real? Wait, you actually came through for me? Does this mean I actually have to let go?

How do I make sure I'm enough? How do I make sure you don't fall out of love with me?

"Just keep being you."

Huh?

But, you gave me worlds to wear on my wrist and the shirt off your back. Told me to release my anxieties and fear with tiger's eyes. Gave me the support of the steel elevated railways on East 98th and you don't request anything in return.

What the fuck am I supposed to do with that?

So every day, you'll just show up?

The way you said you would?

Holding me up and holding me down?

And you just love me?

Like this?

Even when I'm hungry?

Even when my coworkers piss me off?

Even when I'm mad at you?

Baby, how the fuck do I write about that?

Cold Brew

I remember blue shoes with gold studs
I remember white lace
I remember selfies in my boyfriend's car after the whole ordeal
I remember being happy, I remember feeling proud of myself and not really caring who was and wasn't.
I remember drinking, dancing, and decorating
I remember 22, 23 and 24
I remember getting the keys to my first classroom and my apartment.
I remember tequila shots, taco nights, and time alone
I remember starting to teach elementary school
I remember telling my boyfriend that I didn't deserve what he was dishing
I remember blocked numbers and the first time I was called a bitch
I remember being in love, I don't know when I wasn't anymore.
I remember feeling loveless and lustful looking at him
I remember thinking he was perfect and there was no way I could get him
I remember getting him

I remember Hennessey and Honey iced tea from the Chinese food store and thinking Hennything could happen.
I remember not giving a fuck that it was Valentine's Day (for the first time ever)
I remember feeling overwhelmed, overworked and objectified.
I remember realizing people can really be two-faced bitches
I remember not being able to breathe
I remember feeling a funeral in my brain.
I remember abandoning everything I thought I believed in
I remember sleeping…a lot
I remember middle school
I remember feeling successful for the first time in a year
I remember falling in love again, just to later wonder if I was wrong to believe it again
I remember feeling at peace, prepared, and positive.

Milton Keynes UK
Ingram Content Group UK Ltd.
UKHW020707150124
436059UK00017B/892